Whispers
from
Wildlife

Marcus Bach

DeVorss & Company, Publishers
Box 550, Marina del Rey, CA 90294

ISBN: 0–87516–628–8
Library of Congress Catalog Card No. 90–61424

First Edition

Printed in the United States of America

Acknowledgments

Page drawings by Barbara Barth
Cover design by Shari Gurstein
Scanning the quippery by R. H. Grenville

Fondly Dedicated
to
Marguerite R. Beale

Contents

The Induction Session

Have you ever been analyzed by a chipmunk? Whether or not, these sessions with Charlie will prove instantly beneficial, especially since mind-curists and psychologists have finally confirmed what most of us have always known: *there is a remedial power in imagination, therapeutic value in fantasy, healing in humor, and wonder-working miracles in the art of imagery.*

Typical of the fervor of this oncoming cycle of better health through mental magic and objectification was a news release headlined: POWER OF IMAGINATION EXCITES PSYCHOLOGISTS. It reported how an analyst was cured of migraine headaches by a mermaid named Ethel, how a frog called Horace prescribed effective remedies for patients with emotional obsessions, how a dog, Skippy, psyched out the root cause of psychosis in a stubborn client, and how a gremlin told a systems analyst, ''I am your connection with the Infinite Cosmos!''

All along, here was Chipmunk Charlie, my personal shrink, one of the most skilled and innovative masters of creative ideations for the id, completely left out of the scenario. Charlie—an achiever so empathic, a technician so suave and subtle that I urged him, against his will, to go public.

While most analysts are loners and secretly nurse their own ambivalences, Charlie had at his chirp-and-call a staff of entrepreneurs from members of the Animalia-Familia Intergroup, every last one of them a graduate of the UNDERBRUSH UNIVERSITY OF PSYCHIATRIC SKILLS. All had been trained to look at problems not as part of a multi-problem or as a thread in a network of symbolic dysfunctioning, but, rather, as challenges offering opportunities for personal growth through the witty use of Charlie's quippery, a scanner which he chooses to call WHISPERS FROM WILDLIFE.

The Sessions with Charlie

Each morning on the patio
A chipmunk hops up on my toe.
I feed him thirteen cherry pits;
He fills his jowls, and there he sits.

It came to me as no surprise
To learn that he could hypnotize.
Nor could I possibly have missed
His skills as psychotherapist.

Without a moment's hesitance,
He was my shrink in residence.
Seeing past each problem's nexus,
Guiding me through my complex-es,
Tracing all my traumas,
Hearing each confession,
He took me into therapy,
Thirteen cherry pits per session.

Nature was his treatment room,
Wildlife was his staff;
With those who helped effect a cure,
He split his fee in half.

For private consultations
I visited his hutch,
A hillside combination
Of corridors and such.

The walls of his reception room,
Scraped clean from earthy hills,
Were papered with citations
From the best diploma mills.

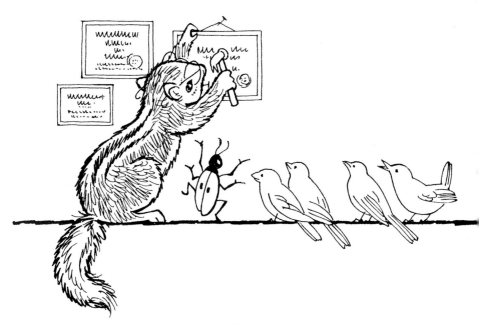

I dubbed him "Chipmunk Charlie,"
Since he liked alliteration,
And his psychiatric services
Were his avid aspiration.

So the wildlings of the Selkirks,
In the Province of B.C.
Joined with my furry analyst
And finally "de-shrinked" me.

In the valley of the Selkirks,
Where they cleared my psychic snarls,
They refer to him respectfully
As simply "Doctor Charles."

The Therapy Appointments

Self-Doubt

Why Am I Here?

High against the eastern sky
An eagle whispered "Who am I?"
The sun came up as if to say,
"Leave that to me; enjoy your day!"

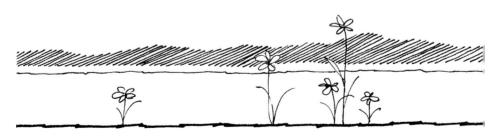

The News

Do the headlines depress you?

No matter what the headlines say,

The robin sings at break of day;

His happy outlook quite confirms

His trust in nature, and in worms.

Insatiable Desires

Would you settle solely for an RV?

A fox to be happy needs room to roam 'round,

While a hedgehog wants only a hole in the
    ground;

But for someone like you and someone like me,

We must have both, or we don't feel free.

Faith

Do you have the will to believe?

Every evening, just for fun,

A loon sends his call to the setting sun,

And in the morning, just for luck,

He calls again and the sun comes up.

Outsiders

Do you fit in?

The aphid, unlike you and me,

Is outlawed by society;

And yet, just like me and you,

Roses are its favorites, too.

Self-Esteem

Do you get your thrills vicariously?

A tiny wart on the back of a toad

Had never walked; it always rode.

"I get my exercise," it said, half joking,

"In the ups and downs when the toad
is croaking."

Enterprise

Are you ambitious?

A bright-eyed flea with a high I.Q.,

A Ph.D. and ambition, too,

Opened a school to educate fleas

How to recognize pets with pedigrees.

Progress

Do you have a hard time keeping up?

An aged inchworm broke down and wept

While calculating the mile he'd crept;

The reason for his sad travail

Was the change-over to the metric scale.

Practice

Do all your efforts seem unworthwhile?

A cuckoo bird in a forest glen
Cucked louder than his fellowmen;
As his prize, the cuckoo flock
Housed him in a cuckoo clock.

Persistence

Do you have determination?

A fleck of moss the size of a dime

Spread into the garden though it took some
time.

Few saw its beauty save now and again

Some poet, or elf, or exponent of Zen.

Orientation

Do you lack inner vision?

The Fifth World is a world so fair

I've learned to see it everywhere,

But through experience more and more

I see it best through my back door.

Decisions

Is making a choice impossible for you?

Hamsters, contrary to creation,

Have yielded to domestication.

They made their choice, it seems to me,

Between freedom and security.

Competition

Do you like to compete?

A nightingale who sang by day

A long and lovely roundelay

Justified his strange position

By saying he disliked competition.

Self-Confidence

Do you question your capabilities?

A sage hen with the clear surmise

That "sage" meant she was specially wise

Played the part so very true,

They made her dean of Sage Brush U.

The Complexity of Life

Does it have you confused?

Kokanee are funny fishes,

They build their lives around three wishes:

To climb the rapids, make love and spawn,

With which, content to die, they're gone.

Togetherness

Do you sometimes feel too *close?*

One thing that can't be said for another,

A sandburr sticks closer than a brother;

But it seems to be one of its tricks

That as it sticks it also pricks.

Compensation

Think your mistakes were all for nothing?

A ladybug in a beechnut tree

Was felled by a blast of DDT;

It was quite sad, but now we see

It immunized her progeny.

Eccentricities

Do people think you're strange?

A stinkbug on a leafy tree

Was being buzzed by a bumblebee;

What to the bee was a fearful smell

Served the stinkbug very well.

Learning

Think it's impossible?

A homing pigeon never left its nest

Because it couldn't tell east from west.

Its mother arranged for it to train

By roosting all day on a weathervane.

Criticism

Do you think you're misunderstood?

"As for the mole, let's gun him down;
He's diggin' holes all over the town!"
It's good the rifle shots all missed him;
He now directs the subway system.

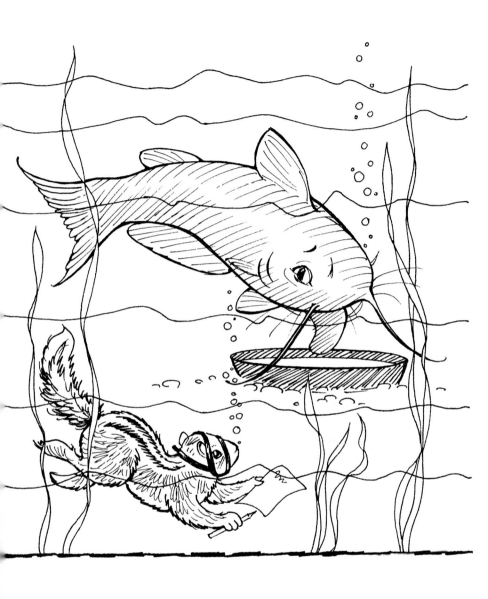

Daydreaming

Do you fantasize too much?

A catfish in a muddy stream

Fantasized a bowl of cream.

He lapped it up and said, "Meow,"

But finds his tummy's aching now.

Travel

Could you stand staying home during your vacation?

A tick is neither slow nor quick;

He finds his place and there he'll stick.

For travel he cares not a jot;

His life revolves around one spot.

Accomplishments

Do you work only for the salary's sake?

A clever horsefly, feeling cocky,

Made believe he was the jockey.

He wore his silks, the race was won;

Though no one knew, he still had fun.

Parenting

Do your children sometimes drive you crazy?

A potato bug in a luscious patch

Watches with pride as her babies hatch.

But soon tears gather in her eyes;

The kids are screaming for french fries.

On Ancestry

Do you long for a better bloodline
in your family tree?

A Canadian mosquito, skilled and sure,

Stung the Queen on her royal tour.

There now are mosquitoes in northern B.C.

Claiming royal blood in their progeny.

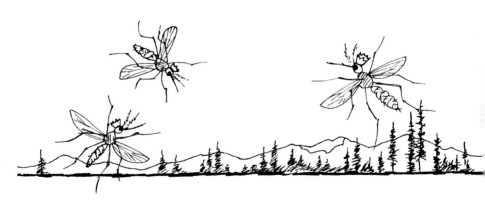

Having Fun

Is enjoying yourself important?

Long, long ago, like yesterday,

The dinosaurs came out to play,

But never having any fun,

They just gave up and now they're done.

Meditation

Do you get your inspiration vicariously?

Every morning to greet the dawn

A dove glides softly to my lawn;

It lives next door in the swami's home

And just comes round to chant its OM.

Children

Do your kids seem rebellious?

If you were a baby kangaroo
In a pouch for a month or two,
Wouldn't you want to jump about
The very moment *you* got out?

Relationships

Do you hesitate making a commitment?

A porcupine engaged for mating

Found the matter of quills excruciating;

Prospects of the affair so thoroughly winced her

She remained the rest of her life a spinster.

Depression

Does it seem the hard times will never end?

To a caterpillar, weeping, sad,

Dangling from a milkweed pad,

Something whispered, "Do not cry."

"That sounds," he said, "like a butterfly!"

Knowledge

Do you ever use all that book learning?

A weaver bird from way out west
Made it big with the IRS.
He showed his flock how they could learn
To sew loopholes in their tax return.

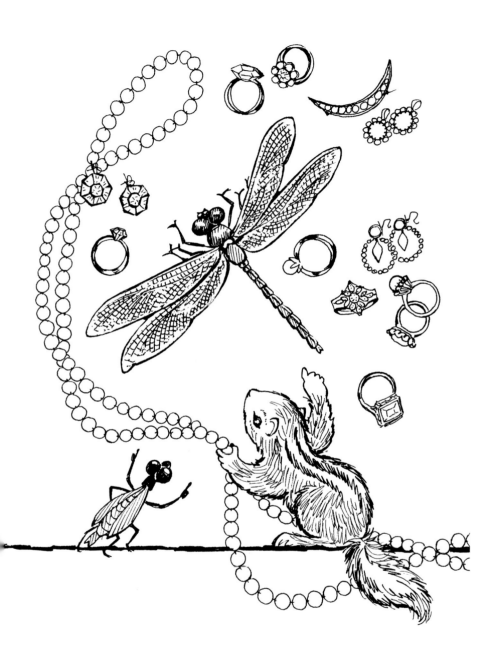

Beauty

Think you can get by on looks alone?

A dragonfly with silver wings,

Two ruby eyes and some golden rings . . .

Who could ask for anything more?

But there she lies in a jewelry store.

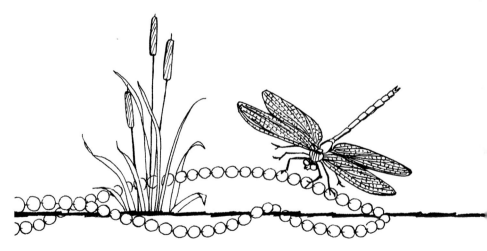

Mortality

Do you worry about dying?

The lemming comes and the lemming goes,
And why he does it nobody knows.
But when one looked at me, I knew;
I came and I'll be going too.

Obesity

Do you overeat?

A tapeworm in a supermart

Hitched a ride on a shopping cart;

It had been a glutton to the point of crisis

But changed its style when it saw the prices.

Distractions

Finding it hard to focus?

Penguins think it very nice

To do their mating on the ice.

They don't complain if the wild wind sings;

They have their mind on other things.

Safety and Security

Are you over-protective?

A foxy fox built a house of rocks

And bolted the doors with double locks.

Security, he said, was his inspiration,

But he died one day of suffocation.

Expanded Consciousness

Are you psychedelically inclined?

A spider under LSD

Entwined his head in his webbery;

His faithful wife got the knots untied

A breath and a half before he died.

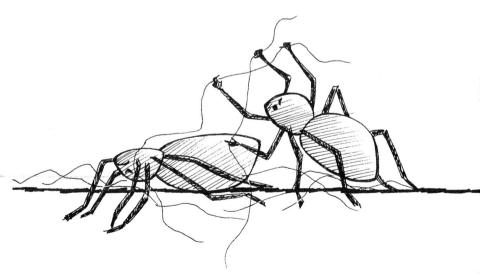

The Environment

Does it challenge your concern?

A band of glowworms, tails aflame,

Heard an angry voice exclaim,

"Man the spray gun! Save the park!"

It is quiet now and very dark.

The Meditative Arts

Are you easily confused?

A baby dolphin confessed to me
He took a course in advanced Tai Chi;
But now when he sees the symbol thing
He doesn't know if he's yang or "ying."

Guilt Complexes

Do you feel the need for absolution?

An aging ostrich with time on her hands
Proceeded to bury her head in the sands;
Asked why she assumed this awkward position
She said it was penance for sins of omission.

Investing

Has your broker ever broken your heart?

Little sheep, little sheep, without any cares
Why did you challenge the bulls and the bears?
Little sheep, little sheep, where are you now?
I told you never to trust the Dow.

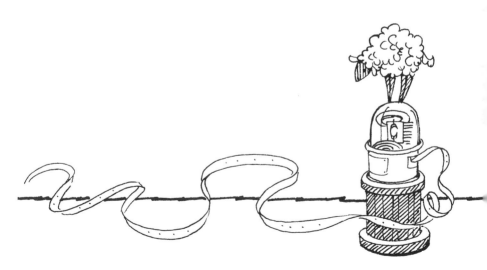

Self-Confidence

Do you feel you aren't dressing the part?

A penguin with a medical degree
Dressed different than those in his colony;
His pants were short, his coat was cute,
He called it his malpractice suit.

Peer Pressure

Do you measure up?

A ringtail goose, quite well read,

Wept each night when she went to bed,

Till a gander told her, "With such lovely legs,

You don't have to lay any golden eggs."

Glamour

Are you worried about your looks?

A lady owl once won a prize
For having the loveliest feminine eyes;
The judges just didn't care a HOOT
That she used mascara to look so cute.

Worrying

Are you under stress?

A baby phoenix had just bedded down,

When the fire alarm went off in town.

The sleepy bird began to snore,

Having gone through all of this before.

The Question of Propagation

Are you concerned about the exploding world population?

Rabbits were once a happy breed

Adding and multiplying to fill their need,

But now with condoms and the pill

Things have gotten rather still.

Acquiring Quietude and Calm

Do you often feel as if you had ants in your pants?

To repair a rent in his baggy pants

A conniving bear hired carpenter ants.

The ants refused by thinking hard

And reporting they had no union card.

The Art of Aging

Are you willing to keep your limbs limber
to stave off getting stiff?

An infant gibbon much like me

Loved to swing from tree to tree;

Now much older and much like him

It's hard to go from limb to limb.

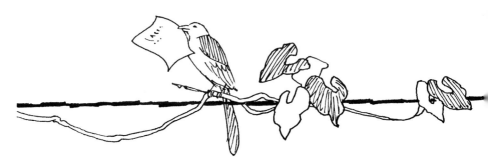

Coming Clean

*When you say you "bank on it" can you trust
your conscience to be your guide?*

A jobless pack rat without any cash

While prowling around in a pile of trash

Found some campaign money laundered so
    clean

He cashed it at par with the party machine.

Abandonment

Can you handle loneliness?

Every morning, rain or shine,

A sparrow sits on my telephone line;

I feel for him, poor lonely thing,

As I wait, alone, for my phone to ring.

UNITY
CHURCH OF THE FOOTHILLS
1111 WEST BADILLO ST.
COVINA, CALIF. 91722

14.00

2 65 $ 1 3 . 8 5